Passacaglia and Thema Fugatum in C minor

Edited by
Charles-Marie Widor
and Albert Schweitzer

Johann Sebastian Bach

32178 r×

T0044600

JOHANN SEBASTIAN BACH

Passacaglia and Thema Fugatum in C minor

EDITED BY
CHARLES-MARIE WIDOR and ALBERT SCHWEITZER

G. SCHIRMER, Inc.

DISTRIBUTED BY

HAL•LEONARD®
CORPORATION
7777 W. BLUEMOUND RD. P.O. BOX 13819 MILWAUKEE, WI 53213

6

8

Thema fugatum

U.S. $6.99

ISBN 978-0-7935-4565-0

G. SCHIRMER, Inc.

DISTRIBUTED BY

50799